Angela Rippon's
Learn with
Victoria Plum
BIRDS

Purnell

HELLO! WOULD YOU LIKE TO MEET MY FRIENDS THE BIRDS? THERE ARE OVER EIGHT THOUSAND DIFFERENT TYPES OF BIRDS AROUND THE WORLD, BUT I'M JUST GOING TO SHOW YOU THE ONES I KNOW BEST, WHO LIVE AROUND MY HOME. OTHERWISE, WE'D NEVER FINISH THE BOOK! IT'S QUITE HARD TO DESCRIBE HOW BIRDS BEHAVE, BECAUSE WITH SUCH A LOT OF BIRDS, THERE'S BOUND TO BE ONE THAT DOESN'T BEHAVE LIKE ALL THE REST! STILL, I'LL GIVE YOU A START IN LOOKING AT BIRDS, AND THEN YOU CAN GO AND MEET SOME FOR YOURSELVES—BECAUSE WHEREVER YOU LIVE, THERE WILL BE SOME TO LOOK OUT FOR!

With a little of her fairy magic, Victoria has made the birds
come alive out of the pages of a book about the Great Wood.

Wood pigeon
Green woodpecker
Tawny owl
Brown owl
Chaffinch
Great tit
Cuckoo

Town and Country

Rooks often break large twigs off trees, and carry them carefully back to strengthen their nests.

Thrushes like a tasty meal of snails. They hold the shells in their beak, and hit them against stones until they break.

Male *blackbirds* are black, with orange beaks. But the females are brown all over!

A *sparrow* is the bird you're most likely to see on a bird table or in a bird bath.

Crows are very intelligent birds. They'll eat any kind of food, and work out clever ways of getting it!

Starlings gather in huge, noisy flocks, often on city rooftops.

BIRDS SING TO ATTRACT A MATE, TO WARN THEIR FAMILIES OF DANGER AND TO TELL OTHER BIRDS, WHO ARRIVE UNINVITED, THAT 'THIS IS MY PATCH!'. WHEN YOU HEAR A BIRD SING, TRY TO SEE IT AND IDENTIFY IT. GRADUALLY YOU'LL LEARN TO RECOGNISE COMMON BIRDS' SONG.

The bigger birds, which hunt and kill smaller animals, are called *birds of prey*, because they 'prey' or feed on other creatures.

Coots eat plants and small water animals, like tadpoles.

Mute swans run along the water before they take off, and ski to a halt when they land.

The *moorhen*, when it needs to escape, can swim away underwater.

IT'S HERE AT THE SEASIDE THAT YOU'LL SEE THE RIVER MEETING THE SEA, AND I'VE CHOSEN THIS SPOT BECAUSE IT'S HERE THAT YOU CAN SEE MY FRIENDS THE RIVER BIRDS, AS WELL AS THOSE WHO LIKE THE SEA.

Beaks

Robins, *wrens*, *sparrows* and *tits* have small, pointed beaks for catching and eating insects.

Finches, such as the *chaffinch*, have beaks that are tough and thick—just right for crunching up small seeds.

Rooks and *starlings* have beaks made for stabbing into the soil, to catch the worms and grubs they like to eat.

Wading birds, like the *heron*, have long thin beaks which are very useful in muddy and watery places.

Hunting birds, such as *hawks* and *eagles*, have big hooked beaks for tearing their prey.

Ducks, *swans* and *geese* use their flat beaks for sifting their food from the water. You'll see them on rivers.

CAN YOU SPOT WHICH BIRDS HAVE THE DIFFERENT TYPES OF BEAK?

Feet

Partridges, hens and *pheasants*, like most birds, have three toes pointing forwards, and one pointing backwards, to make perching easy.

Swifts have all four toes pointing forwards, for clinging to walls and cliffs. Almost always seen in flight, swifts do not need 'perching' feet.

  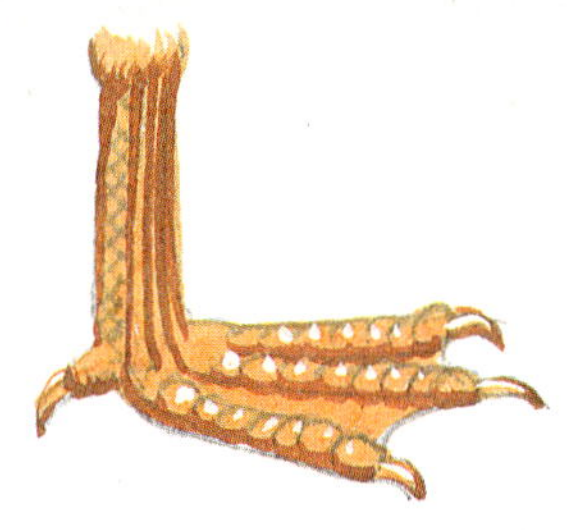

Birds of prey, such as *owls* and *kestrels*, have very strong feet with long talons, for grasping their prey.

Woodpeckers have two toes pointing forwards and two pointing backwards, for gripping the bark of trees as they peck.

Water birds like *ducks* have webbed feet. They are useful as paddles for swimming.

EVERYTHING ABOUT BIRDS IS DESIGNED TO HELP THEM FLY. THEIR BONES ARE HOLLOW, SO THAT THEY DON'T WEIGH MUCH, AND THEIR SMOOTH BODIES, COVERED IN FEATHERS, ARE 'STREAMLINED' SO THAT THEY GLIDE EASILY THROUGH THE AIR. FLYING LOOKS EASY —UNTIL YOU TRY IT. EVEN THE BIRDS HAVE TO LEARN, AND THERE ARE SOME ANXIOUS MOMENTS FOR THE PARENT BIRDS WHILE THE BABIES ARE FINDING OUT HOW TO DO IT.

Birds' wings are rounded above and hollow underneath, so that by flapping them very fast, the bird can get air to lift it up into the sky. Birds' wings aren't all the same —*owls* have fluffy feathers for silent flight, *eagles* have wide wings for hovering, and *swallows* have swept-back wings for fast flight.

On a bird's body some of the feathers are fluffy and soft. They are called *down*, and keep the bird warm. The wing and tail feathers are stiff and long, for flying. If you try stroking a feather the wrong way—from the tip downwards —you will find that the soft pieces tend to stick together. This is because they have tiny hooks on them, to link the strands together. When you see a bird preening itself, it is straightening out these parts of the feathers so that they lie flat.

Tail feather

Down feather

Wing feather

Nests

Birds build their nests in springtime, in all sorts of different places, and in many different ways.

Many birds build a cup-shaped nest, wedged in the branches of trees or large bushes. The *blackbird* that Ben saw was off to make a nest like this, of dry grasses and dead leaves, held together with mud.

The *long-tailed tit's* home is really cosy, with lots of protection from the weather. It is oval, with just a small hole for a door, and a neat covering of spiders' webs all over it.

The *chaffinch's* nest has a built-in duvet, for it lines its mossy nest with feathers.

Sparrows, *house martins*, *starlings* and *jackdaws* nest on the walls or under the roof eaves of houses. You can always tell a house martin's nest, because it is made entirely of mud.

One bird which makes no nest at all is the *cuckoo*. Instead, it lays just one egg in another bird's nest. When the baby cuckoo hatches out, it turns the other eggs out of the nest, so that its foster parents have only the intruder to feed, thinking that it is their baby all along!

The Migration Mystery

As the seasons change, many birds travel across the world to find the weather that suits them. Many of Ben and Victoria's friends face a dangerous journey, often thousands of miles long, twice every year. It's called *migration*. The birds travel together in flocks; that way they have a better chance of surviving the long trek.

In the spring, *swallows*, *warblers* and many other insect-eating birds come to Britain to raise a family. They are guided here partly by the Sun and stars, flying thousands of miles from the heat of Africa. When autumn comes, and food gets scarce, they have to fly south

again in search of warmer places with better food supplies.

While the insect-eaters are flying away, other kinds of birds, like *geese* are on their way here from the bitterly cold lands farther north.

The birds which fly the farthest are the *arctic terns*. They nest near the Arctic circle, but travel across the other side of the world, to the Antarctic, in search of food during winter.

Experts are able to map migration routes by ringing birds and recording their travels. But no one knows *exactly* how birds find their way on their long journey. Many go back to the same nesting spot year after year!

Watching birds

You'll need a good bird guide, so that you can identify the birds you are watching. Early morning is the best time to watch, because it is then that they feed. You can encourage birds to come to your garden by putting out food and water for them. But it isn't fair to do this if you have a prowling cat waiting to pounce.

Keep a notebook just for writing down the birds you see. You should also write the date when you see them, and where they were. If you don't know the name, write down as much as possible about the bird's appearance. This will help you to look it up later.

Watch carefully when you see a flying bird. Did it fly in a straight line, or did it soar, and then drop? Was it hovering? Look at the shape of the bird as it flies, because this will help you to find out what it is.

Feeding birds through the winter is one way in which you can help to make sure that birds survive.

There is a junior branch of the Royal Society for the Protection of Birds, which does much to protect birds of all kinds.

Send a stamped addressed envelope for more details about the Y.O.C.—and maybe you can get your friends interested in it too!